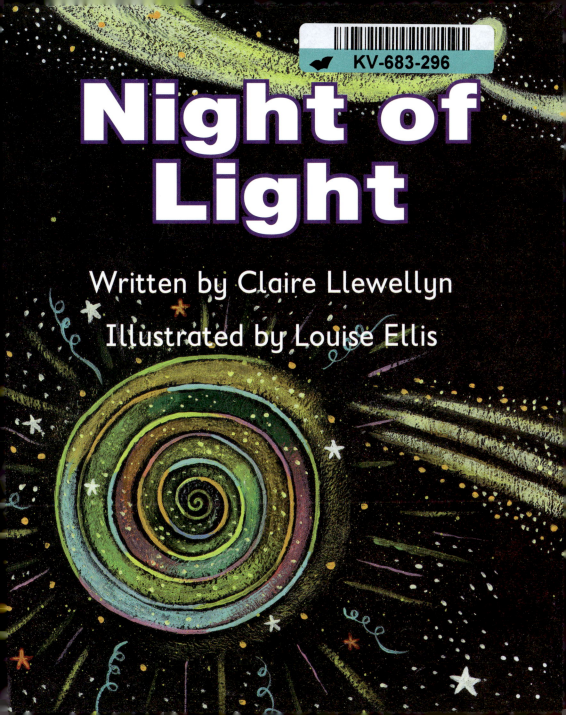

Night of Light

Written by Claire Llewellyn

Illustrated by Louise Ellis

Black night,
cold and bright.

2

3

Light the fire on Diwali night.

5

Sizzle, fizzle,
whoosh, whizz,

Crack

BANG

whoosh, swoosh, crackle, fizz!

7

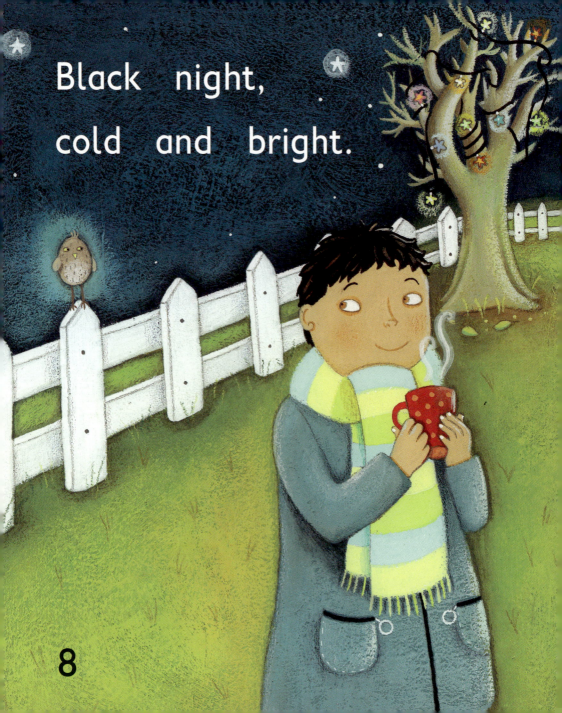

Black night,
cold and bright.

8

Light the fire...

11

on Diwali night.